Literally Speaking

The MERLD World Survival Kit

Parent-Teacher Workbook

Cie L. Hosmer

Edited by Jen Kocher

DEDICATION

This workbook is dedicated to all the parents and teachers who work together to create a classroom environment where the literal child can process information and learn efficiently.

ACKNOWLEDGMENTS

I would like to thank all those who have made MERLD World a parental resource and support network for their kids with mixed expressive receptive language disorder. It would be impossible for me to name the hundreds of families who work so diligently to help others understand what MERLD is and how to support it.

I especially wish to thank my editor, Jen Kocher, who has been someone that I can rely on for straightforward feedback and valued friendship. Thank you for seeing what I could not and for your continued support of MERLD World.

WHY I AM GIVING YOU THIS WORKBOOK

You are an integral part of my child's interdisciplinary team. I know that your day is spent with many children with many unique needs. That is why I am giving you this workbook. By helping you understand how my child processes information, I hope to promote better understanding of MERLD and bridge some gaps that may occur in my child's education.

PLEASE NOTE

DISCLAIMER: This workbook is simply a tool for facilitating child-specific information between parent and teacher/school. Any child-specific information written therein is meant to be confidential.

MERLD World Survival Kit is not responsible for any misuse of information between any parent, teacher or school.

My goal as his parent is to keep the lines of communication open. To this end, here is my latest contact information:

Email: _____

Phone: _____

THANK YOU FOR TAKING THE TIME TO GET TO KNOW MY CHILD BETTER

MY CHILD AT A GLANCE:

My child's name is: _____

My child prefers to be called: _____

My child has mixed expressive-receptive language disorder or MERLD (also MRELD). It is a processing disorder.

This is not a "textbook" rendition of mixed expressive receptive language disorder, expressive language disorder or receptive language disorder. You won't find any treatise here—only practical tips and insights into my child's way of processing information.

As my child's parent, I understand that the key component to better family living is education. Our kids spend much of their waking hours with you. MERLD can be difficult to address as the challenges are unique at home and in the classroom.

Other important notes:

Co-morbidity: two or more chronic disorders or conditions present in a person. For instance, someone with MERLD may also have ADHD.

You also may find that some students may have some social and/or behavioral issues related to the difficulties in processing information on the fly.

In the classroom, it can get very frustrating being unable to process multi-step instructions. Example: steps to a math problem such as long division

I will discuss with you any co-morbidity, social or behavioral issue that I have noticed with my child. If you notice anything new or have any concerns, please contact me so we can further discuss. Thank you!

My child's MERLD diagnosis has indicated that:

_____ The receptive deficit is dominant

_____ The expressive deficit is dominant

WHAT IS MIXED EXPRESSIVE RECEPTIVE LANGUAGE DISORDER (MERLD)?

MERLD is an acronym for mixed expressive receptive language disorder. This means that my child, your student, has both expressive disorder **AND** receptive disorder.

Simply:

Expressive disorder: inability to express all or some of their thoughts to others.

Receptive disorder: unable to understand part or all the message they receive from others.

Combine both, and you have a student who is a very visual, literal, hands-on learner needing accommodations to process information successfully.

Mixed expressive receptive language disorder (also known as mixed receptive expressive language disorder) is not:

+ a disability (disability is the legal term, disorder is the medical term) These terms are often used interchangeably.
+ autism, although it may be a characteristic that children with autism may have.
+ always known by the child. Students with MERLD may or may not understand they have MERLD and what it is. To the students who do not know what MERLD is, school as a learning and as a social situation can be quite disconcerting and even frightening.

Students with MERLD need you to understand that their brains are wired differently. One analogy is to think of the MERLD brain as a computer with its data scattering in all directions before coming together on the screen to be understood. Like operating systems, this can take more or less time depending on the individual, the data and working memory issues.

IMPORTANT

Everything you teach your MERLD student is going into his brain; but, your student has mild to severe difficulty **RETRIEVING** that information, connecting that information with what is happening in the classroom and creating a response on the fly. This can be very frustrating for your student and for yourself when you are on a tight schedule.

Once the connection is made--usually by time and learning style accommodation--those connections tend to stay with the student with patience and practice. Be very literal. Rephrase as necessary.

Remember this above all: the child with MERLD is a **NORMAL** child with age appropriate emotions and needs. Your student will carefully assess the class surroundings, scope you out as a teacher and react accordingly.

To Sum Up:

➤ MERLD is a communication processing disorder.

➤ MERLD is not a learning disability. It is a language disorder. However, under IDEA, it may be legally classified as a disability. It may fall under speech or language impairment or specific learning disability. It may qualify a child for accommodations under Section 504.

➤ MERLD is not autism.

➤ MERLD is not unmanageable.

DID YOU KNOW?

How many words per minute an adult or a child typically processes?

Adults: 160 to 180 words per minute

Children: 124 to 140 words per minute

"Depending on their age, studies show a child's central nervous system can process speech with reasonable accuracy when words are spoken at a rate of approximately 124 to 140 words per minute. The problem is, the typical adult rate of speaking is 160 to 180 words per minute. Many teachers and parents unknowingly speak too quickly to children, and then complain that they aren't listening."

Source: Ray Hull, audiologist, Wichita State U. Professor, Communication Sciences and Disorders, Audiology/Neurosciences

Wichita State News: "Professor Ray Hall co-authors new book *The Art of Communication*" April 20, 2016

Teacher's Notes:

_____

_____

_____

_____

_____

_____

_____

_____

_____

_____

Parent Notes:

_____

_____

_____

_____

_____

_____

_____

_____

_____

_____

INSIGHTS INTO MERLD BY GRADE

PreK through Grade 1

Many students with MERLD have been recently diagnosed. Some will not have IEPs yet. Some will be just beginning speech language and other therapeutical intervention.

You will likely see less social interaction, lots of parallel play and a "hanging back" in group communication like circle time. Some kids will need extra help with lunch. Be very concise and visual.

> My child may need very literal directions presented in 1-2 steps. Beyond that, my child may have difficulty processing multi-step instructions.

.

What PreK and First Graders

May Need You To Understand

- Most of us don't know what MERLD is.

- I can't make friends because I can't get what everyone is talking about.

- Too much noise makes me crazy.

- I sit back because I am trying to follow along and can't. Everyone is talking too fast.

- I want to learn.

- I want to please you and let you know that I am trying to learn.

- I need you to be patient with me.

- I sometimes feel unsafe to talk in class. My family understands me. I need time to feel safe and not rushed.

- I may or may not tell you the truth if I am scared. I may tell you I understand when I really don't, because I don't know what else to do.

Here's How You Can Help Your Student

- Don't attempt to explain MERLD. That is the parent's responsibility.

- Look at facial cues.

- Many MERLD kids seem aloof, look out the window or out the door or past you when you talk. It may seem that they are not listening; but, they are attempting to process what you are saying. If you give a lecture or instructions too fast or use multi-steps to explain something, your MERLD student may feel lost.

- Speak normally, but concisely. Ask if he understands. Explain instructions one step at a time. You may need visual or tactile helps.

Teacher's Notes:

_____

_____

_____

_____

_____

_____

_____

_____

_____

_____

Parent Notes:

_____

_____

_____

_____

_____

_____

_____

_____

_____

Grades 2 through 4

The Transitional Grades

Many kids with MERLD have been in speech language and other therapies for a time. They are a bit more interactive, still hanging back and assessing. They are learning to manage what

> My child is carefully watching you and his classmates. He is learning how to process information in a manageable way. Multi-step problems are still an issue.

processing skills are best for them. Parents are likely focusing on not only their school education, but follow-up education at home. Learning the activities of daily living and how to manage spontaneity and nuance are paramount from here on out.

What You May Notice:

Your MERLD student may not "get" social cues.

Graphic organizers are great for helping keep multi-step assignments in check.

Some students with MERLD are very social and others are not.

Working memory may be limited. What a student "gets" one day, may be gone the next. What is happening is that although the information is in the brain, MERLD makes it difficult to pull that information out in a timely way. Many times it will seem that nothing is connecting.

It helps to be very engaging, literal, visual.

Teacher's Notes:

_____

_____

_____

_____

_____

_____

_____

_____

_____

_____

Parent Notes:

_____

_____

_____

_____

_____

_____

_____

_____

_____

Older grades

Many children "grow out" of MERLD--that is, they learn how to *manage* input and output--their processing skills have matured to a point where they can better keep up with their grade level.

Not all students will reach this point and continue to have processing problems through adulthood, which may affect their social interactions. Biologically, MERLD does not "go away."

Middle school and high school students may seem to regress from time to time. Tween and teens may seem forgetful, need more sleep, are preoccupied with social lives, the usual woes. This may seem to exacerbate their MERLD and processing may take longer.

Teacher's Notes:

_____

_____

_____

_____

_____

_____

_____

_____

_____

_____

_____

Parent Notes:

_____

_____

_____

_____

_____

_____

_____

_____

_____

_____

MERLD at a glance:

Every child with MERLD is unique as their personalities, brain pathways and emotions are unique. Many were and are late talkers.

Many require occupational therapy for handwriting issues.

Some may have stronger expressive skills.

Some may have stronger receptive skills.

Some are gestalt learners. Some have co-morbidities (other conditions) that make learning and social interaction extra challenging, especially in the early years of education.

Q and A with 14-year-old LT, diagnosed at age 4 with MERLD

Question:

If you could tell a teacher one thing to help you in the classroom, what would it be?

Answer:

The scariest thing in all my grades was when the teacher called on me. Everyone talks at once or the teacher talks too fast and expects me to answer questions when I'm still trying to understand what is being said in the classroom. My brain won't always work quickly enough to give an answer. So I would just not talk.

MERLD AND THE IEP OR SERVICE PLAN

My child is more than his IEP or Service Plan.

IEPs tend to hone in on specific issues and not address the holistic issues of MERLD. This is understandable, as my child's interdisciplinary team needs to assess written goals for my child.

However, my child holistic needs include:

(parents please check all that apply)

___My child is literal and takes every word at face value.

___My child learns best visually. Graphic organizers are very helpful.

___My child learns best kinesthetically. An abacas will aid in math.

___My child needs patience. Rushing through assignments or adding time constraints are frustrating to the child who has difficulty processing instructions.

___My child's expressive processing is worse than his receptive processing. He understands but cannot get the words out in the proper context or order.

___My child's receptive processing is worse than his expressive processing. Scrambled data needs to be unscrambled and it takes time to accomplish this.

___My child may parallel play until he feels comfortable engaging in interpersonal play. This may or may not come to pass.

___My child may not participate in circle time. He may simply listen and attempt to understand what is happening and why he is in a circle.

___My child will likely not understand nuance. Be literal. Be specific. Don't talk in generalities or use idioms, jargon, or expect that facial expressions or common gestures will be understood readily.

___My child will likely not "get" jokes. But my child may smile or laugh to fit in, depending on the age group.

___Idioms will escape my child. "I need another assignment like I need a hole in my head." You will get shocked or quizzical looks!

___My child needs routine, literal instructions and simplicity, not "dumbing down." My child may not test well on timed or written tests. He may do better on oral tests. Most MERLD kids are average to above average intelligence. They just need time to process what is being said and time to find the right words to express what they need to express.

___Multi-step directions are very difficult for my child—especially math. If you need my child to complete multiple steps for an assignment, please be literal in explaining the steps, use a graphic organizer or write down each step. Even a task like taking the green book from your desk and running it down to the office and telling Mrs. So-and-so that I need the white book instead, will be daunting. You may have a child who will see multiple green books and not know which one to take, who will "run" to the office because you said to do so and forget what he ran down to the office for and what to say. Keep it simple. Hand the green book to my child, say please walk this down to the office. Mrs. So-and-so is waiting there to give you a white book. Bring it back to me. Thank you.

___My child's facial expressions are very telling. Furrowed eyebrows and blinking eyes may mean that processing is very difficult and he is holding back tears of frustration.

Please contact me if you have any questions regarding my child and his processing issues.

STRATEGIES THAT HELP STUDENTS WITH MERLD

General Classroom Aids

Graphic organizers and storyboards are wonderful tools that will help my child stay on task and able to process more efficiently.

Parent Insight:

These are some educational aids that have proven helpful for my child at home or in my child's past classroom experiences:

_____

_____

_____

_____

_____

_____

Sample Strategies for Teachers

Processing Larger Amounts of Simple Data

Target Grade: 5 or 6

Processing Issue: Faced with too much information.

Framework: birthdays

Details: months, days.

Problem: Child had to answer questions about the birthdays and graph them.

Possible Solution Steps:

- Print two full-year calendars. One with just months, no days. The other with both months and days.

- Put a check mark or a tick mark under birthdays that appear in each month on the month only calendar.

- Do the same for the month and day

calendar.

- Count the marks for each month or each day, write the sum next to the month and circle it to bring it to the forefront of attention.

This makes answering questions like how many birthdays fall in October or how many birthdays are on March 3 easy to find instead of sifting through 20 kids' names and birthdays through a list. It also makes graphing birthday totals easier.

It gives them organized visuals and takes away the overwhelming processing of too much information.

Chunk it.

Where should your MERLD student sit in the classroom?

It depends on the personality of the student and any other conditions that merit special consideration. Talk to the parent and watch the student during noisy times and times of interaction.

Ideas to think about:

Reduce distraction: allow your student to sit in the second or third row of the class, off to the side, not directly in front of your desk. Think in terms of the L-shape. Why not the first row? The first row can be especially intimidating to a MERLD child. The L-shape arrangement gives the benefit of being close, but also insulated by other students who like to pay attention. Having your student off to the side gives them the illusion of "breathing room." A little space to gather thoughts. Right in front of your desk can feel intimidating.

Circle Time--When Your MERLD Student Won't Sit Still or Join In

Grade Target: PreK-2

Problem:

Circle Time can be very intimidating or confusing to a child with MERLD. First, the entire classroom (or a portion thereof) sits in a small area--in today's smaller classroom that usually means a confined space surrounded by the desks, paintings drying, hanging on wires strewn throughout the room, etc.

Circle Time is usually meant as a relaxing, transitional time for students and teacher, but often it makes MERLD kids feel closed in, surrounded by too much visual and auditory stimuli. This can cause frightened kids, confusion or tuning out.

Try this:

When was the last time you sat down on the carpet with your students? Get down and look from their line of sight. What do you see? It can be like a bug in the grass for a student with MERLD. Remember that Rick Moranis movie "Honey I Shrunk the Kids?" Up in the rocker, from your point of view, it's tidy and in control. Down where the child sits is a whole new "ecosystem" for the child, packed with other kids fidgeting, talking, etc. The child sees all the toys, books, crayons in boxes. You get the idea. For some kids, this is too much. Creating a less busy space for circle time may help your student feel more comfortable processing the information/story, etc. you are trying to convey.

Remember, MERLD students often have trouble with more than one or two things going on at once. Sensory overload.

PROBLEM:

Many MERLD kids have trouble with comprehending math concepts.

STRATEGY:

Focus on the quality of the homework problems completed (or attempted), not on the quantity of the problems completed.".

HOW TO ACCOMPLISH THE STRATEGY:

Step 1: Accommodate the child by reducing the quantity of math problems. If the mainstream class is completing 20 long division problems, give the MERLD child 10, but give them all 20 so that they have the option to work the problems.

Step 2: Make sure that you don't try to fit 20 problems on one side of a sheet of paper. When a child has comprehension issues, too many math problems clustered together can look like Greek. Space them out and give the child plenty of room to work them.

Step 3: Use special paper as a math graphic organizer so that your student can focus on one step at a time. Multi-step problems are very often difficult for MERLD kids to process.

One that has columns for the numbers under the radical is best.

Math Anxiety: Grade Target: 6

Protractors--measuring angles
Problem:
No matter how much you instruct a student to match up the point of the angle with the point of intersection at the 90-degree mark and the zero line, many MERLD kids will have difficulty placing the protractor correctly. Even if they get the placement correct, protractors have many lines and come in many colors. Those lines and colors are distracting. Which line do they look at? And how do you measure the other angles if you have, say, a triangle?

Try this:
Simplify protractor use by using a clear protractor with grade-appropriate markings. Elementary school kids work best with larger, clear protractors that are open in the middle. This gives a clear view of the markings and the

angles. Make the instructions more visual by dotting the intersection of 90-degrees and the zero line; use a marker to line the zero line for guidance."

To measure angles of a triangle or other shape-- let your student know that they are in control of the angle. They can turn the paper in any direction to make placement of the protractor easier--as long as they meet intersection point to angle point and line up the bottom of the angle to be measured on the zero line.

NOTES

**Thanks again for taking the time
to get to know my child.**

Made in the USA
Monee, IL
03 April 2021